MY FIRM FOUNDATION

TRANSFORMATIVE TIPS FOR THE GOD-SEEKING, COLLEGE READY STUDENT

STERLING D'VON SHIPP

My Firm Foundation

Copyright © 2024 by Sterling D'Von Shipp

All rights reserved. Published by

Blue Café Books for
www.carladupont.com
Atlanta, GA

Printed in the USA.
ISBN: 979-8-218-41423-8

All rights reserved. In accordance with the U.S. Copyright Act of 1976, the scanning, uploading, and electronic sharing of any part of this book without the permission of the publisher constitutes unlawful piracy and theft of the author's intellectual property. If you would like to use material from the book (other than for review purposes), prior written permission must be obtained by contacting Sterling Shipp at www.sterlingdshipp.com.
Thank you for supporting the author's rights.

Credits
Editorial: Carla DuPont
Cover Design: Garrett Myers

DEDICATION

I dedicate this book to my family, church home, and community that took the time to pour life into me throughout the years. Thank you! I am more grateful than you will ever know.

FOREWORD

In the writing of *My Firm Foundation: Transformative Tips for the God-Seeking, College Ready Student*, Sterling D'Von Shipp, more than captures his lived experiences as a college student; yet, without compromising his faith and spiritual formation. As you walk through the various seven (7) chapters, you will walk in a sense of discovery of self. You will appreciate the real lived experiences and challenges of life itself. More so, in this context, there is an authentic appreciation of life as a college student who celebrates the maze of joy and pain, challenges and victories, throughout the course.

"*My Firm Foundation: Transformative Tips for the God-Seeking, College Ready Student*" (My Firm Foundation) is creatively written in a manner that allows the reader/student to be drawn into the work in a participatory context, all while speaking through the lens of trusted wisdom and experience. The reader/student will celebrate the fact that they are able to connect with the "Personal Tips" from the author, explore the dynamics of the author's "Take Home Tips", and most supreme, embrace the fact that there exists the sections entitled "Tips to Put into Action." This unique method and structure will definitively grab the attention and engage the reader to explore the praxis of Sterling's lived experiences.

You will applaud the notion that the author, Sterling D'Von Shipp, remains on the continuum of his spiritual formation journey as he constantly reminds the reader of the integrity of his faith. This is a concept that permeated each chapter in many ways. This is critical, especially in our current context whereby social media with its various means and content, far too often offer a counter narrative than that of the author. *My Firm Foundation* encourages the reader/

student in multiple ways, and becomes a major influence in life, especially during the years of formal matriculation, college years. Sterling's goal is to never compromise the pillars of a Firm Foundation.

The book allows you to "start where you are." It is an easy read, and instructional. It offers encouragement via homework assignments. The work is intentional and non-judgmental, and will not judge nor vilify those who may be wrestling to grasp a sense of balance in life. You will be inspired to read, engage, and ultimately celebrate your growth and transformation. Ultimately the goal is to share your confidence and success with your peers and others. The key to this transformative process is the supernatural power of PRAYER. The author clearly infuses prolific trust and commitment to the dynamics of prayer throughout the read.

Finally, there is much to be said about this writing.

However, space and time are of the essence. Nevertheless, I'd like to intentionally give one particular example from a chapter that, in my humble opinion, serves as a prototype of the essence of *My Firm Foundation*. I will extrapolate an example from chapter four (4) entitled "The Complexity of Comparison." The author upholds that "God's standard is *supreme* and *superior*, compared to our faulty human standards." What a Word!

In a world where many thoughts and ideals evolve and change with rapidity, and truth bends, for many, in order to formulate a socially constructed phenomenon that seeks to debunk the tenants of the aforementioned Firm Foundation, the reader/student is being encouraged to avoid comparing oneself for a sense of acceptance. Comparison is potentially dangerous as you seek positive transformation while traveling the maze of life, regardless of the context. You have cherry picked a book that will meet you on your journey, in a real way.... Good traveling!

Rev. Dr. Tony F. Drayton

B.A., MTh., MDiv., DMin.,

Lead Pastor of St. James Church, Riviera Beach, FL

Holy Spirit, You and I will change the world.

Have your way!

I surrender all I have to you, day by day.

TABLE OF CONTENTS

1 ..... THE FIRM FOUNDATION 1
2 ..... THE EVOLVING RELATIONSHIP 10
3 ..... THE LIE THAT TRIES TO DEFINE YOU 22
4 ..... THE COMPLEXITY OF COMPARISON 31
5 ..... THE TRUSTED FAMILY 37
6 ..... THE TEST OF LOVE & TEMPTATION 45
7 ..... THE CHRIST MINDSET 55

INTRODUCTION

We all live by a certain set of ideals, beliefs, and values, something that keeps us going, even when we do not want to press forward.

Many nights, usually in deep thought, I have asked myself, *What is my foundation? Who or what truly gives Sterling meaning?* I am a family man. I love and respect family too much to not include them in my reason for pressing forward. They truly mean more to me than I could ever articulate.

With that being said, **there is something deeper.** To cut straight to the chase, the answer is **Jesus Christ.** I am not referring to religion, I am not referring to an abstract concept that trends during Easter and Christmas. I am talking about a true, loving, real relationship with God's only begotten son.

There is a quote I live by, that I wrote for myself a couple years ago and it goes as follows, "Be selfless enough to ALWAYS find time to **pour LIFE** into someone else." This book is that opportunity for me to pour LIFE into you, the reader. When I speak of LIFE, I am talking about Jesus Christ, **My Firm Foundation.**

As you read this book, I want you to pray, take notes, ask questions, and share any gems you find with someone else. Although this book is intended for students going to college, any and everyone can be blessed by what is within the pages of this unique writing.

MY FIRM FOUNDATION

TRANSFORMATIVE TIPS FOR THE GOD-SEEKING, COLLEGE READY STUDENT

1
THE FIRM FOUNDATION

"JESUS FREAK!"

"BIBLE THUMPER!"

"FAITH FANATIC!"

"HOLY HYPOCRITE!"

"HOLY ROLLER!"

As I lay on my bed writing this chapter, I cannot help but think of so many other names that I have heard people throw at Christians on social media, say face-to-face and behind our backs. Keep in mind, I am currently 22 years old. I know for a fact more insults could be included here.

Putting all of the name-calling aside, I am personally not bothered by the names that much; it honestly makes the journey that much more enjoyable. I wanted to share a glimpse of what it may sound like when you walk onto a college campus and take your faith walk with Jesus Christ seriously. College is already a trying time as you navigate things like learning the campus, making new friends, joining clubs/organizations, and choosing classes – not to mention growing close to God and understanding what I mean when I refer to 'The Firm Foundation.' Let me give you an easy introduction to **Jesus Christ, 'The Firm Foundation.'** Standing strong on Jesus and what He says is where it all begins.

If I were to say taking your faith walk with Jesus Christ, Son of the One and True Living God, on campus would make your life easy and delicate, like drifting on a cloud, I would be lying. Then, this book would serve you no purpose.

As I mentioned previously, faith in Jesus is a journey and it must be personal. Personal? What do I mean by personal? I am glad you asked. I mean having an intimate relationship with Jesus for yourself. Your parents could have dragged you to church every day of the week or enrolled you in the best Catholic, Baptist, or Seventh Day Adventist school growing up. **Until you know Jesus for yourself,** participating in those activities were just a wheel spinning in the religious machine.

Many people go to church, but how many really know God? Many people quote scriptures on a daily basis, but how many live true to the same scriptures they quote? God despises the self-righteous living of a HOLY HYPOCRITE. I am surely not the one to judge you or anyone else; that is God's responsibility. I am just here to have an honest engagement with you, my friend. Having this personal relationship with Jesus is a rough ride filled with tests and trials. Only those who have accepted Jesus into their lives will be able to produce fruit sweet and good for eating.

What do I mean by this? Let me help you out.

In the *Holy Bible*, which I sometimes refer to as 'scripture,' the Lord Jesus Christ says, "Yes, I am the vine; you are the branches. Those who remain in me, and I in them, will produce much fruit. For apart from me you can do nothing" (John 15:5 New Living Translation).

Long story short, if you are connected to the true, living, and good vine, you will produce true, living, and good fruit - Jesus is the true vine. If you are disconnected from the true vine, you will produce whatever you are connected to. Think about it!

Imagine a table-top drink dispenser that holds punch and lemonade which you have seen at banquets and parties. The liquid in the drink dispenser is the source, the spout is the channel, and the liquid that pours out into the cup, is the product. If we are connected to ungodly sources, ungodliness is all that we will produce. Likewise, if we are connected to

God, we will produce justice, mercy, and humility. If that does not help, check out this example. While you are in college and you chill with a group of friends that go clubbing every weekend dragging you along every time, or maybe you are the one dragging them along, clubbing will evolve into the fruit that you produce, it will become your product. Not only clubbing, but some of the other things that are aligned with being out late at night in such a capacity include: hooking up, excessive smoking, excessive alcohol consumption, and developing brain fog. Like the saying goes, 'you are what you eat,' let me create my own: 'you produce what you are constantly attached to.'

Choose wisely → Choose Jesus.
QUESTION: How would you define SUCCESS? Especially after dwelling on what I just put on the table of your mind.

I would personally define success as:

1. Making God proud
2. Being an inspiration to those who look up to me
3. Being a servant-leader to my future wife, children, and family/lifelong friends.

However you define success and however you picture yourself in the future, make sure to put yourself in check and re-evaluate what and who you are connected to. I am rooting for you to make the wisest decision of your life! I sincerely encourage you, from the bottom of my imperfect heart, to choose the author and finisher of success, the King of Kings and Lord of Lords, and even more impactful - the LOVER of your soul, **Jesus Christ.**

Material success is what we want, but eternal and everlasting connection to God is what we need.

Thankfully, if you connect to Jesus Christ as

'**The Firm Foundation**' that CANNOT fail, you will know choosing Jesus Christ is **eternally** the CORRECT decision.

TAKE HOME TIPS

Jesus Christ is *The Firm Foundation*, and standing strong on Jesus and what He says is where it all begins.

Just like the saying goes, 'you are what you eat,' let me create my own, 'you produce what you are constantly attached to.'

However you define success and however you picture yourself in the future, make sure to put yourself in check and re-evaluate what and who you are connected to.

2 THE EVOLVING RELATIONSHIP

What is the first thing that comes to mind when you think of the words, 'evolving' or 'evolution?' Do you think of science? I am sure you do not think of Christianity or a relationship with God. The more I understand my faith journey, the more I understand that everyone is on a different road, at a different time, in a different way, with a different capacity, and with a different trajectory. The good news is, the Lord Jesus Christ said in scripture, "I am the Way, the Truth and the Life. No one can come to the Father except through me" (John 14:6 New Living Translation).

Take this not so random question for example, What does a wealthy financial advisor in New Jersey and a Georgia bus driver both have in common? They both can **truly seek the Lord initially, want to have a relationship with Him, and receive everlasting salvation instantly** - but grow in the Lord at entirely different rates! Let us say each of them did what scripture says to do, that is, 'confess with your mouth that Jesus is Lord and believe in your heart that God raised Him from the dead, and you will be saved" (Romans 10:9-10 King James Version).

Awesome! They both are now a part of the family! They belong! They are forever embraced in the body of Christ.

The only difference is that one of them reads their Bible, calls on the name of Jesus, cares and prays for the sheep (people) of God - while the other person does nothing. They both are a part of the family, but their relationships with God are evolving much differently. It is not up to me to say which one is "doing better." Again, that is for God to decide, but I know this for sure – God loves them both and He can handle them both in a **JUST** and **FAIR** way, because He is a **JUST** and **FAIR** God.

How will you decide to kickoff your evolving relationship with God? Maybe you have already decided to make Jesus Christ your Lord in the past... that is FANTASTIC! **Welcome home!** - You are a part of a family that **LOVES YOU**, no matter what the world says about you. Your relationship may look very different from someone who has just made that life-changing decision to follow Christ.

If you are brand-new and do not know what to expect, to you I also say, "**Welcome home!** - you are a part of a family that **LOVES YOU**, no matter what the world says about you. **Accepting Jesus** is the greatest decision you could ever make in your life – you will not regret it."

Your individual journey will be unique, it will be rocky, it will even be scary at times. God can handle your worries and concerns. Quick tip! Do yourself a favor and lay your daily stressors at the door of His heart; pray and seek Him in everything you do. Find a sincere, loving, and humble fellow believer to pray with, as you dive into the Holy Bible, His perfect word.

When it comes to my evolving relationship with God and college planning - one of the best decisions I ever made in my junior and senior year of high school, was **sincerely** talking to God in my own unique way. When I prayed, I spoke aloud, and usually paced around the floor like a nervous, young middle school boy, waiting to see the girl he had a crush on at school – such a simple time in life. I remember speaking aloud and telling God boldly that I would not attend any college He did not want me to attend. My final decision would not be made based on girls I liked or friends' decisions. I wanted my decision to be entirely based on what God said and what He said alone. This was my attempt at doing God's Will.

The reason I wanted to do God's Will is because He knows what is best. One of the differences between God and myself is that I can only see the situation right in front of me. To be honest, sometimes that picture is not totally clear. But I know He holds the future, and I am learning, day-by-day, to trust Him more and more.

Ultimately, through many days and nights of prayer, research, and confirmation from God, I chose to attend one of the most rewarding public universities in the State of Florida, and a top-ranking university in the United States, as an undergraduate. **GO GATORS!** I am grateful and honored that God did what He did, and I have not regretted the decision at all, no matter how uncertain college can be.

A quick tip I would give to someone who is looking to grow their relationship with God, during a stressful and exhilarating time such as going off to college, would be to **start where you are!**

I literally want you to do your best to pause how you react to the distractions of life and start opening up to God, speaking aloud with your mouth. I advise finding an appropriate Bible verse and reading it aloud. While you are reading this Bible verse aloud, open your heart to God and let Him know how you feel. I usually start with "Dear Heavenly Father…" but that is just me. Begin by acknowledging Him and how AWESOME and EXCELLENT He is. Turn your focus and thoughts away from yourself and the current circumstance, and focus for a moment on how capable He is to handle your situation.

After greeting Him, I go into the desires of my heart and speak openly, plainly, just He and I - **with no distractions.** During times like these, I will put my phone on 'Do Not Disturb,' or will walk away from a crowd of people.

On a side note, although I start my prayers off with "Dear Heavenly Father," because that is exactly what He is, He is also named **God Almighty, Sovereign Lord, King of Kings, Alpha and Omega, The All-Merciful One, Adonai, Jehovah Jireh, Abba Father, and so much more.** Although He may have many names that describe His essence, clearly our human language is limited in its description of His excellence. The mind-boggling part about it all is, this same perfect God desires a closer relationship with you and I, no matter where you are and no matter what you have done.

PERSONAL TIPS JUST FOR YOU

START WHERE YOU ARE.
SPEAK ALOUD.
OPEN YOUR HEART TO GOD.
SPEAK FROM WITHIN, WITH NO DISTRACTIONS.
BE RESPECTFUL AND ENTIRELY YOURSELF.

Your relationship with God is constantly evolving, there will be days when you will not do any of this and will just "go with the flow." As much as I wish I could tell you that it does not happen, not wanting to pray happens to **ALL** of us. It happens to new believers, it happens to seasoned disciples. Not wanting to pray happens to preachers and pastors, and it happens to college students with all of the right intentions. Yet, we will press on and depend on Him for guidance because He really does care that much about you **AND** your prayer life.

This fighting urge not to pray at all, is the very same urge that will **distract you** from praying **when you decide to pray**. Distractions are frequent, fatiguing, and foolish. Since this is the case, it is all the more clear why we always need to be honest with God in this evolving relationship. We are not perfect, God is. That is why we need to connect, listen, and OBEY. It is easier said than done, but it is possible through Him.

Are you having trouble with distractions in your life?

If you are struggling like the rest of us, give this very brief scripture an honest listen. Scripture says to, "pray without ceasing" (1 Thessalonians 5:17 King James Version). Now, if you read that extremely short verse and get a little nervous about praying without ceasing, we should understand that 99.9999% of us cannot pray 24 hours a day, 7 days a week for 365 days a year without doing anything else. Obviously, we must eat, sleep, work, and accomplish many other things. This scripture, like all scripture, is getting at something much deeper. It is signifying that we should always be in constant contact with God, reading His word throughout the day, talking with Him (also known as seeking His face), and allowing the Holy Spirit to live in you and guide you, once you have believed in Jesus Christ, Son of the Living God.

Do yourself a favor and meditate on the Word of God, always praying to God and letting Him lead you in how your relationship with Him should go. I have benefitted greatly from doing this myself, and I hope you challenge yourself by doing the same.

TAKE HOME TIPS

When I say, **"start where you are,"** that means start opening up to God, speaking **ALOUD** with your mouth.

Distractions are frequent, fatiguing, and foolish. Since this is the case, it is all the more clear why we always need to be honest with God in this evolving relationship.

1 Thessalonians 5:17 (King James Version) says, "Pray without ceasing." This scripture signifies that we should always be in constant contact/connection with God.

THE LIE THAT TRIES TO DEFINE YOU

3

With expectations so high, oftentimes set by ourselves and others around us, we constantly hear, whether internally or externally, that our mistakes define who we are. Let me be extremely clear right here, right now, **THAT IS A LIE!**

Rather than sugar-coating what is a lie, what is a "half-truth," and whatever other soft language being used today, I am not here to be politically correct, I am just here to speak the truth.

The belief that we are the epitome of our worst mistakes and the belief that we cannot be forgiven or set free from our failures in life **IS A LIE.** Join me, as I gladly tell you why.

No matter how annoying or difficult, it is our right and responsibility to own our mistakes by acknowledging that they happened, bringing them before God, and leaving them there for God to guide us through them.

In all transparency, it was painfully humbling for me when I learned that **I earned my first D+ ever** on a report card or transcript. As an honor roll student my entire life, never earning a C or anything below that, on a report card or transcript previously, let me just tell you that was a college experience I will never, ever forget. The key to getting through this time was realizing I needed to forgive myself, learn from my mistakes, and most importantly, take it before God. When I took this concern before God, I was simultaneously **emboldened and terrified.**

Going to God boldly in prayer is a sign of maturity in the faith because it shows that you know your place. Listen to this. When we go to God in all sincerity, we are exemplifying a position of dependence on Him. Going to Him with a feeling of trembling and terror is both human and understandable. Having fear is human nature, but letting it control our minds and lives is not representative of a child of God maturing the way we should. So, when I first prayed about this concern, I probably cried out, asked so many questions and felt overwhelmed with doubt. Yet, the more I mature and grow, I understand He is in control, and I need to focus more intently. I would advise anyone in a similar situation, **not to trust the process, but put your trust in the One who holds and knows the process – Jesus Christ.**

In my circumstance, the lie running around in my head a million miles a minute, taking up space and confusing whatever clarity was left, sounded something like this, "You just made a D+. I guess this is the new normal for you, Sterling. Don't expect anything better than this from now on."

The reason this was a lie and **always will be a**

lie, is that I know from where my strength comes. I do not allow my mistakes to hold that much power over my head and define who I am and who I will be, **and neither should you.** Some might say, "That is easy for you to say, you have faith." My response would be, "Trust me, it is not easy for me to say at all; but, it is easy for God to handle. My faith is not in me; it is in Him."

If you are having trouble picturing how you could apply this kind of faith in your life, **you have realized the very definition of faith.** You will not know how strong or weak your faith in God is until you have put it to the test. It is easy for anyone to **say** how strong their faith is. It is easy to **say** how much they believe what they heard from a Christian YouTube Short, or **say** what they remember reading from a random Jesus post on Instagram or X (formerly known as Twitter). Faith strengthens with experience and experience makes prayer worthwhile.

If you are like me, initially asking the question, "Does God really hear my prayers?" Let me respond as clearly as I know how, "YES!" God hears our prayers. Even more than that, God takes to heart what you have to say — there is a difference. I personally know God listens to my prayers because He answers in only the way a loving, sovereign God would — in His way and in His perfect time.

Shortly before I earned that D+, I began to pray a constant prayer that God would strengthen my trust in Him. Needless to say, He tested my trust by allowing me to be in a situation I had never been in before. God truly has a sense of humor. Although I honestly hated earning the D+ in this college class, I am grateful the experience happened because I am now able to say it significantly **strengthened** my faith in Him.

You see, another lie I told myself initially was

that the letter grade defined who I was, while God was saying to me, **"If you have faith and trust in Me, you will be defined by what I say you are."** Scripture says, "Do not fear. I have redeemed you. I have summoned you by name. **You are mine**" (Isaiah 43:1 New International Version). Scripture also states, one of my grandmother's favorite scriptures, "and we know that all things work together for good to those who love God, to those who are called according to His purpose" (Romans 8:28 New International Version). I love this scripture because it seems so generalized, yet it is so precise. The scripture **does not say** all things **are good**..., the word of God says, **"all things <u>work together for good</u>..."** meaning it might not initially look good, be good, smell good, or sound good, but will **work together** for good to those who love Him, to those who are called according to His purpose.

In college, there will be plenty of

opportunities to believe in just about everything. In a sense, the world is yours and literally lives at your fingertips. With all of this to consider, let me leave you with a short line of caution that I believe will make an impact as you read this book today.

Read carefully, this is **JUST FOR YOU.**

"Do not believe the hype that the lies may speak, trust in the One who is there for you when you are weak. Your past mistakes do not define your essence or your entire life, God is more than able to remove the guilt, stress, and looming strife."

Sterling D'Von Shipp

TAKE HOME TIPS

We constantly hear, whether internally or externally, that our mistakes define who we are. Let me be extremely clear right here, right now, **THAT IS A LIE!**

Yes, God hears our prayers, but even more than that, **God listens** to your prayers - there is a difference. He actually cares.

Faith strengthens with experience and experience makes prayer worthwhile.

4 THE COMPLEXITY OF COMPARISON

If we are honest with ourselves, we all compare ourselves to others from time-to-time. This concept began in many of us from when we were just babies and has continued into adulthood. This is an act many of us fall into the trap of on social media and once it starts, it is very hard to stop. The title of this chapter is aptly named, "the complexity of comparison," because it is just that... **complex**.

Comparing what we have to what others have, comparing where others are in life to ourselves, comparing how tall we are, and comparing how much money we have. It continues with comparing how much status we can obtain, how many likes we receive, how long our relationships have lasted, and the list literally goes on and on. These examples are among the myriad of complexities that extend into your college life. Without going into another exhaustive list of how we operate in regards to comparing ourselves to others, it should simply be stated there are pros and cons to doing it - but the ultimate question is: Where does it get you?

Practically, a benefit of comparing yourself to someone else, is that if you can see the hard work someone is putting into class, studying, sports, playing an instrument, and the analysis gives you a burst of energy to be more productive.

A disadvantage of comparing yourself is that you become internally and seemingly eternally self-conscious, always walking on eggshells, afraid to take a risk out of fear of not meeting the standard set by someone else. Either way you look at it, the art of comparison is complex. Sure, it is noble to have a proper role model and someone to look up to, but the first and foremost role model should be, you guessed it... God.

God's standard is SUPREME and SUPERIOR compared to our faulty, human standards. It is important to understand that comparing yourself with others will do as I always say, "Either put you above someone else in your mind or beneath someone else in your mind." At the end of the day, we will believe what we want to believe, yet we should know, that what God says and knows about us is most important. This begs the question, is comparing ourselves amongst others worth it in the grand scheme of things?

Scripture says, "...but they, measuring themselves by themselves, and comparing themselves among themselves, are not wise, (2 Corinthians 10:12 New King James Version)." This scripture signifies that we are not wise to seek perfection among people who are imperfect. On a deeper, spiritual level, if you are seeking something that can fill the God-sized crater in the depths of your soul, only God will be sufficient. On a practical level, if you are looking for a role model, more specifically – someone to emulate and follow, Jesus is the primary target. Then, your personal hero can come next.

The moral of the story is, where does comparing ourselves get us when we all have imperfections and flaws that we cover up from each other? God is the ultimate standard and yes, other people can fill in as practical, earthly role models, but we know that nothing can compare to *'The Firm Foundation'* – **Jesus Christ.**

TAKE HOME TIPS

On a deeper, spiritual level, if you are seeking something that can fill the God-sized crater in the depths of your soul, only God will be sufficient.

God's standard is SUPREME and SUPERIOR compared to our faulty, human standards. It is important to understand that comparing yourself with others will, as I always say, "Either put you above someone else in your mind or beneath someone else in your mind."

THE TRUSTED FAMILY

One thing I have learned in my 22 years of life, is that family does not only consist of those who are related to us by blood. Sometimes, people who are not blood-related can be more like family than those who are. Respectfully, I make this statement having been blessed with a loving community of people who are always pouring life into me, ever since I was a child. I have also been blessed to have a loving blood-related family that instilled in me at a young age faith in God, being a part of the Church (Body of Christ), serving others, and loving your neighbor.

Whether or not you have a background in loving the Lord from your childhood, you can always **start where you are** and **come as you are** to God. Finding your very own trusted family in college is important because they can provide you with what you cannot get on your own. Leaving my home and going off to college four hours away, one of the first things I did was pray I'd be able to find a loving, non-judgmental, Christian family of believers who loved the Lord and that I could grow in God with. Like I said before, God listens to our prayers. Soon after I prayed that prayer, He answered me, although in His own way and in His own time.

In my first semester, I was able to cautiously grow into a Christian family of believers at my university. As soon as I entered their midst, I felt God's love all around me and knew I belonged. Tastefully, the very first song we sang together as a group was, *"just taste and see that the Lord is good."* This experience might look different for everyone. Yet, if you sincerely ask God to lead you to the right people, He will answer you in His way and in His time, without a doubt. You just have to be open and willing to let Him work. When I refer to a trusted family, I am referring to the loving, imperfect, God-respecting, Bible-teaching, non-judgmental people of God who are growing in Christ more and more each day. NOT religious machines. Without going into great detail, **there is a HUGE difference between lovers of Jesus Christ and religious people (religious machines) who participate in religion just for the sake of participating in religion.**

I have been known to speak my mind and tell it like it is. I firmly believe there is no purpose in randomly joining a "religious" Christian group, without praying about it first, just for the sake of checking off a box on your college experience list. Especially when you could be growing in God doing something more meaningful. Prayer is the key to finding the trusted family for you because only God knows where you are to be planted at that specific moment in time.

On one of our spring break trips, the aforementioned Christian campus group and I traveled to the United Kingdom and France. Our main purpose was to have a great time in the Lord, fellowshipping, reading the Bible, absorbing what God had to say to us through our fellow brothers and sisters in Christ, and of course, last but not least, travel, sight-see and eat diverse European food. The most amazing and blessed part of this trip was initially meeting with these saints (other members who believe in the Lord Jesus) in Europe, and being treated like we were blood-related family. The hospitality, the lovingkindness that the Bible speaks about, and the sharing of honest, sincere, and Godly testimony are more profound than I could ever write on paper.

The myriad of experiences on this trip are just some examples of how I know God truly led me to the perfect trusted family, **for me.** As I stated and let me be extremely clear, these are not perfect people, but **they are perfect for me. God always knows what we need and whom we need.**

One additional tip about finding the trusted family is that they truly have to be trusted by you if you plan on growing in God alongside them. Family allows mistakes and errors because they realize they are people as well. A true family will not judge you, but will correct the issue by walking alongside you, guiding you as you all are guided by God together.

Since we all have flaws and oftentimes get off track, the trusted family is there to be a pillar of accountability for each other. Two scriptures from different books of the Bible that both refer to this theme of accountability are 1 Thessalonians 5:11 and Proverbs 27:17. Scripture says, "Therefore encourage one another and build one another up, just as you are doing (1 Thessalonians 5:11 English Standard Version)." In addition, scripture also says, "As iron sharpens iron, so a man sharpens the countenance of his friend (Proverbs 27:17 New King James Version)."

Imperfect as we may be, we need other trusted disciples to help build us up, as God gives the growth and does the leading... if you allow Him.

TAKE HOME TIPS

This experience might look different for everyone, yet if you sincerely ask God to lead you to the right people, He will answer you in His way and in His time, without a doubt... you just have to be open and willing to let Him work.

Family allows mistakes and errors because they realize they are people as well... yet a true family will not judge you, but correct the issue by walking alongside you, guiding you as you all are guided by God together.

Imperfect as we may be, we need other trusted disciples to help build us up, as God gives the growth and does the leading... if you allow Him.

6
THE TEST OF LOVE & TEMPTATION

HOT SEX

GETTING DRUNK

NEW DRUGS

FOOTBALL

LINGERING LUST

CONSTANT CLUBBING

VIDEO GAMES

WORKING OUT

GOSSIPING

TRYING NEW THINGS

MEETING NEW PEOPLE

AND SO MUCH MORE…

Now that I have your attention – let's talk about it!

I am excited. ☺

I would be lying if I were to tell you that in college, none of the things listed will ever skate across your mind. I am also not going to tell you how to live your life, that is not my purpose and it never will be.

With that being said, I will let you know **there is a way to continue to grow in Christ, as all these things listed above are going on around you, on, off, and near the college campus.**

This chapter should be an eye-opener for everyone reading it. If you skip reading it for prideful reasons, you are doing yourself a disservice. I am not saying this out of arrogance, I just do not want anyone to say they did not know that the things listed above would present themselves in their college experience.

Now, it may just be that these things listed above do not occur in every collegiate's life. I standby telling you at least one of those in the list is bound to occur.

I have consistently said these "things," instead of using another term to describe them. They all have different avenues. In other words, each one of these things takes you down a different path than the next. This chapter is titled The *Test of Love & Temptation* because in your college experience, if you take one step out of your dorm or apartment and "live a little," you will be tested in love... you will be tested in temptation, and sometimes both will hit you at the **SAME TIME**. The key to growing in Christ while these things arise is putting what was articulated in chapters one through five into action.

TIPS TO PUT INTO ACTION

- Having the firm foundation – Jesus Christ
- Understanding your ever-growing relationship
- Knowing that your failures **DO NOT** define you (believing what God says about you)
- **NOT** having a comparison mindset (letting God be your primary role model)
- Finding your unique, trusted family

Let me be crystal clear about this point. There is absolutely nothing wrong with God's standard of love. God's standard of love is golden and never failing. As scripture states, "He who does not love does not know God, for God is love (1 John 4:8 New King James Version)."

The "love" that we college students call love is a lot of things… and sometimes it is God's standard of love: pure and righteous. A lot of times the "love" we call love is not God's standard at all, and the difference is quite clear. Without generalizing and painting with a broad brush about collegiate love life, I am going to stay in my lane and simply say if you believe you have found love… take it to God. A way to evaluate if that "love" you are referring to is God's standard of love, is by the both of you praying to God together, humbling yourselves before Him in sincere prayer, and asking for guidance on where to take your relationship and at what speed to take it as well.

On the other hand, temptation is always present, always plotting, and always on the move. Temptation will always present itself to us because, we are weak - even when we think we are strong. Although we may think we are strong without God and think we can resist all the plots of temptation, we will eventually fall, make a mistake, or disobey God. The fact is, if the father of lies, 'the enemy,' Satan himself, was brazen enough to set out and tempt Jesus in scripture... Satan has no problem doing the same to us. As the Lord said to Satan himself in scripture, "Away with you, Satan! For it is written, you shall worship the Lord your God, and Him only you shall serve (Matthew 4:10 New King James Version)."

Our idea of "love" and temptation will come and go. Oftentimes, when temptation disguises itself as "love" is when life gets undeniably hard - yet having a firm foundation in the Lord is a key step to making these temptations flee.

Some might wonder, why did I have football, playing video games, and working out included in the bolded list at the beginning of this chapter. The answer is based on these two words "possible distractions." Hear me out. I love college football and working out; my friends love video games. None of these are inherently wrong, evil, or unholy whatsoever. Yet, we will learn that anything can be a distraction, especially in college, where there seems to be a distraction on literally every corner. Consider this - if you have this gut feeling that you should be spending time with your girlfriend/boyfriend, and instead, you are playing video games from 5-10 p.m. on a Friday night... the video game has gone from a "possible distraction," to a "distraction." More importantly, if you know you should be praying to God, as well as getting into the Bible more, and instead, you are solely playing football with friends and working out **in place of** growing in God, these otherwise "good" things have gone from "possible distractions" to "**MAJOR** distractions."

This is a constant battle, but that's why we depend on God to help us along the way. It is way too hard to deal with on our own, we have to consistently learn how to trust more in Him.

TAKE HOME TIPS

Let me be crystal clear about this point. There is absolutely nothing wrong with God's standard of love. God's standard of love is golden and never failing. As scripture states, "He who does not love does not know God, for God is love (1 John 4:8 New King James Version)."

Oftentimes, when temptation disguises itself as "love" is when life gets undeniably hard. Having a firm foundation in the Lord is a key step to making temptations flee.

More importantly, if you know you should be praying to God, as well as getting into the Bible more, and instead, you are solely playing football with friends and working out **in place of** growing in God, these otherwise "good" things have gone from "possible distractions" to "**MAJOR** distractions."

7
THE CHRIST MINDSET

If this chapter were to have a scriptural theme, it would be the following, "Jesus said to him, You shall love the Lord your God with all your heart, with all your soul, and with all your **MIND**" (Matthew 22:37 New King James Version). If the mind were not a powerful thing, I doubt the Lord would have included it when He was speaking to one of the Pharisees (a powerful and highly revered Jewish leader in Biblical times) in this scripture.

If you have ever heard the saying, "the mind is a terrible thing to waste," as my grandmother says, then you know that the mind is very powerful, yet not indestructible. The brain is tangible, we can physically hold it in two hands, whereas the mind is a phenomenon that exists but cannot be touched with human hands. In college and generally in life, the mind will be tested and sometimes it may "crack." If or when you ever feel your mind cannot take the pressure being placed upon it, seek help from wise counselors, good therapists, trustworthy family, real friends, and above all else, **go to God.**

I would be ignorant and foolish, having earned a Bachelor of Science degree in Health Education and Behavior, while on the pre-medicine track, to tell you not to seek help around you... seek God only and ignore the common sense assistance at your fingertips. To say something like that is not only foolish, it is not based on the word of God. God's Word says, "for as the body without the spirit is dead, so faith without works is dead also" (James 2:26 New King James Version). Faith in God is necessary, it should be a priority, and this will **ALWAYS** be true. In addition to this, our faith in God will be put to the test at times. Using the proper resources provided to us is essential. As long as we realize the Lord God is the **source** and He provides resources, then and only then, will we realize He is the Solid Rock on which we stand and depend.

In order to live with a Christ mindset, we have to set our minds on the things above: heavenly things, Godly things, Christ-like things. We have to choose the Jesus Way. From the music we listen to, to the conversations we start, to the groups of people we surround ourselves with, to the habits we develop, having a Christ mindset, especially in college, will benefit you beyond your wildest imagination. People who see you, and I am talking about people who really see you, will see something in you that was not there or was not as profound. When your mindset is fixed on Christ-like things, which can only come from Christ Himself, things like loving your neighbor who may curse you or turning the other cheek when someone slanders your name, will cause people to notice a light in you. It is so funny to me that everyone wants to shine, and many want to be the light of the world, but many do not understand that the light does not originate from them, it comes from God who lives in us. We only shine bright because He allows it to be so; **some brighter than others.**

Will you shine bright in college, throughout your life or wherever you end up in your career? Will that light be a vain, attention-seeking light (which we all seem to fall into from time-to-time)? Or will your light be a light built on the firm foundation of glorifying the Father? Think about these questions throughout your day, and I will challenge myself to do the same.

TAKE HOME TIPS

If you have ever heard of the saying, "the mind is a terrible thing to waste," as my grandmother says, then you know the mind is very powerful, yet not indestructible.

As long as we realize that the Lord God is the **source** and He provides resources, then and only then, will we realize He is the Solid Rock on which we stand and depend.

It is so funny to me that everyone wants to shine, and many want to be the light of the world, but many do not understand that the light does not originate from them, it comes from God who lives in us. We only shine bright because He allows it to be so; **some brighter than others.**

As we come to a close, I want you to engage in a

prayer that someone I hold dear to my heart and have great respect for, wrote **JUST FOR YOU.**

Dear Father God,

I have made plenty of mistakes, I have sinned, and I have wronged you. I repent and turn away from my sins. I invite Jesus Christ, your son who died on the cross for my sins and rose again from the dead, into my life, to lead me and be my Lord and Savior.

Thank you for showing me that because of YOU, I am able to do more than I have ever thought or imagined. Help me Father to write down in detail, to meditate on your Holy and perfect Word, and to talk with you constantly about how to get ready for this college and career journey. I trust you, Jesus. When I have doubts about committing to the vision that you have set for me, when my mind starts to race and I ask about the who, where, when, and how… prepare me as only you can. Guard me mentally, physically, emotionally, and spiritually. Remind me that changes are going to occur in life. Nevertheless, you hold my future and it is a prosperous one. As I engage with diverse people of different races and creeds, experience unique college events, join organizations and associations, lead me with your loving hand.

Show me day-by-day, moment-by-moment, how to make a commitment to the work of the Lord, as I believe you will establish and order my steps.

In Jesus' name, your beloved child, Amen.

- **Written by my prayer warrior & friend**

INDEX OF SCRIPTURE

CHAPTER ONE: THE FIRM FOUNDATION

- John 15:5 NLT - Yes, I am the vine; you are the branches. Those who remain in me, and I in them, will produce much fruit. For apart from me you can do nothing."

CHAPTER TWO: THE EVOLVING RELATIONSHIP

- John 14:6 NLT - "Jesus told him, I am the Way, the Truth and the Life. No one can come to the Father except through me."

- 1 Thessalonians 5: 17 KJV – "Pray without ceasing."

- Romans 10:9 NIV – "If you declare with your mouth, "Jesus is Lord," and believe in your heart that God raised him from the dead, you will be saved."

- Romans 10:10 NIV - "For it is with your heart that you believe and are justified, and it is with your mouth that you profess your faith and are saved."

CHAPTER THREE: THE LIE THAT TRIES TO DEFINE YOU

- Isaiah 43:1 NIV - "But now, this is what the Lord says— he who created you, Jacob, he who formed you, Israel: "Do not fear, for I have redeemed you; I have summoned you by name; you are mine."

- Romans 8:28 NIV - "And we know that in all things God works for the good of those who love him, who have been called according to his purpose."

CHAPTER FOUR: THE COMPLEXITY OF COMPARISON

- 2 Corinthians 10:12 NKJV - "For we dare not class ourselves or compare ourselves with those who commend themselves. But they, measuring themselves by themselves, and comparing themselves among themselves, are not wise."

CHAPTER FIVE: THE TRUSTED FAMILY

- 1 Thessalonians 5:11 ESV - "Therefore encourage one another and build one another up, just as you are doing."

- Proverbs 27:17 NKJV – "As iron sharpens iron, So a man sharpens the countenance of his friend."

CHAPTER SIX: THE TEST OF LOVE & TEMPTATION

- 1 John 4:8 NKJV – "He who does not love does not know God, for God is love."

- Matthew 4:10 NKJV - "Then Jesus said to him, "Away with you, Satan! For it is written, 'You shall worship the Lord your God, and Him only you shall serve."

CHAPTER SEVEN: THE CHRIST MINDSET

- Matthew 22:37 NKJV – "Jesus said to him, '"You shall love the Lord your God with all your heart, with all your soul, and with all your mind."

- James 2:26 NKJV - "For as the body without the spirit is dead, so faith without works is dead also."

KEEP IN TOUCH!

@Sterling D. Shipp & Sterling Shipp

@sterlingdvon

@sterlingdshipp

www.sterlingdshipp.com

Made in the USA
Columbia, SC
04 July 2024